Welcome To Being Human

An Instruction Book for Every Soul

Children's Edition

By: Jonathan

published

May 22, 2018
FIRST EDITION

ISBN-13: 978-1-942967-57-6

KreativeMinds Publishing
publishing@kreativeminds.net
© 2018 All Rights Reserved

On Planet Earth…

My child, this is what must change.

Part I: A Bedtime Story

PARENTAL NOTE: This story can be read to children of all ages. Parents may even learn something new, too!

{ 1 }

To Be Read To A Child

Once Upon a *Time*.

WELCOME TO BEING HUMAN

Once upon a time, my child, there was only One – one light, one star, one *thing* for everything to become.

PART 1 – ONCE UPON A TIME

This star was infinitely BIG!

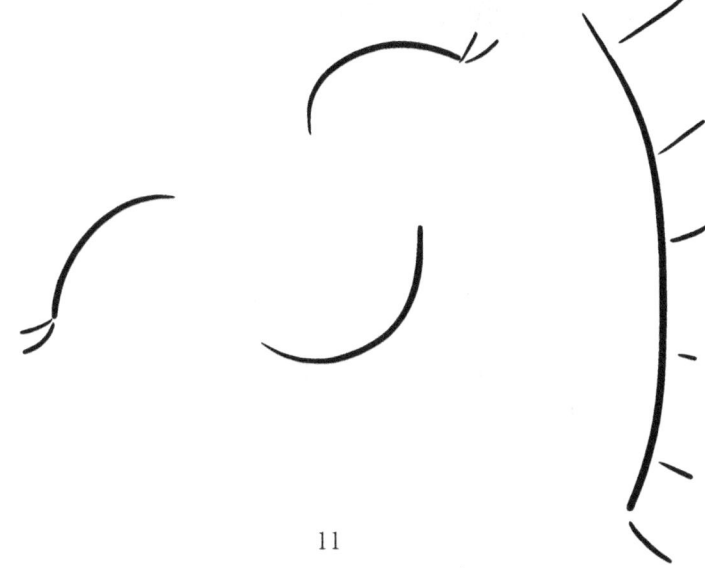

WELCOME TO BEING HUMAN

And infinitely *small*.

PART 1 – ONCE UPON A TIME

Can you see it?

It needed a child to look up at the night sky to SEE it – to experience the wonder every human feels looking up at the stars above.

Can you see the star now?

PART 1 – ONCE UPON A TIME

For how can there be **wonder** if no one is there to see how *magnificent* it is?

WELCOME TO BEING HUMAN

So this ONE became TWO!

PART 1 – ONCE UPON A TIME

...then THREE!

WELCOME TO BEING HUMAN

...then FOUR!

PART 1 – ONCE UPON A TIME

...and SO MANY MORE, until there were too many stars to even imagine!

WELCOME TO BEING HUMAN

It was like a **family!**

And each **star** now had brothers AND sisters!

PART 1 – ONCE UPON A TIME

Each star gave birth to its own worlds where all different forms of life could

experience the wonder and *curiosity* that caused the One to become Two, then Three, and so on.

Each star became *a great mother's* Son – a **Sun** that hugs each planet...

PART 1 – ONCE UPON A TIME

... and hugs each plant, each animal, and each child with so much warmth and **Love!**

WELCOME TO BEING HUMAN

But oh child! Every animal, every creature great and small is **Love** too! Just like the stars and the Sun!

PART 1 – ONCE UPON A TIME

My child, there was never a beginning or an end. There never could be. It was always **Love** –

experiencing itself in every possible way – creating a sense of wonder that could only exist when One was part of a *family*.

You, my child, are a piece of this **Great Love**, with no beginning and no end.

PART 1 – ONCE UPON A TIME

You may be a *tiny human* today,

but this was not your beginning,
and it will not be your end.

Being human is just the briefest of moments of an experience of a **Love** *so grand!*

PART 1 – ONCE UPON A TIME

So when you look to the stars above at night...

...or see the *Great Mother's* Sun during the day...

PART 1 – ONCE UPON A TIME

...know that *being human* is about being caught somewhere between the stars and HOME.

It's learning to see **Love**, experiencing *Wonder*; but most importantly, learning to become **Love** once again.

PART 1 – ONCE UPON A TIME

Once upon a time, there was One. This One was *Wonder*. This One

was **Love**. This One is YOU, my child... and now you know!

Have magical dreams tonight.

You are **Love**, my child. You are *the One.*

Part II: How The Star Became Two, Then Three, THEN MORE!

PARENTAL NOTE: The first portion of the story should be easy for a child learning to read, but the second portion may require some help. This is as it is intended – a story for children and parents together.

{ 2 }

For A Child Learning To Read

The Story of One.

WELCOME TO BEING HUMAN

Once upon a time...

...there was One.

PART 2 – THE STORY OF ONE

One became Two.

Then Three!

PART 2 – THE STORY OF ONE

Then Three became...

Four!

My Child!

Behind those Four, were Four more!

PART 2 – THE STORY OF ONE

So how many does that make?

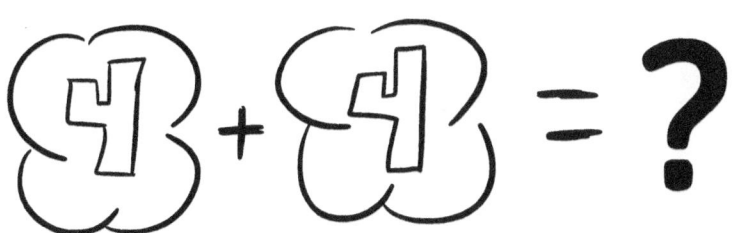

Four... Five... Six...
Seven... **Eight!**

PART 2 – THE STORY OF ONE

But, my child, there is One more!

But where....?

WELCOME TO BEING HUMAN

Surprise!

PART 2 – THE STORY OF ONE

Inside, is number Nine!

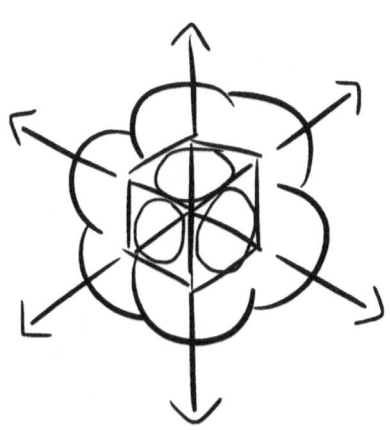

But oh, my child...

On Earth only Seven can be seen.

PART 2 – THE STORY OF ONE

Can you see the Seven?

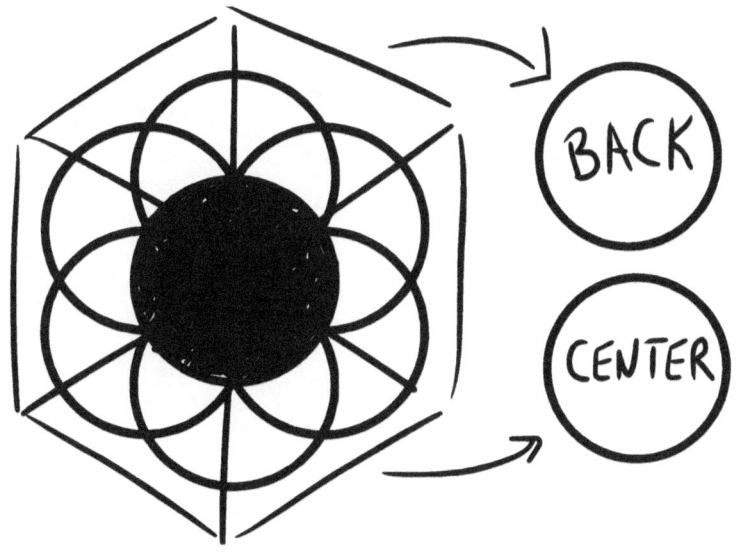

... and Two hidden?

WELCOME TO BEING HUMAN

They make the colors of the rainbow!

PART 2 – THE STORY OF ONE

They make the sounds of music!

They turn thoughts into words!

PART 2 – THE STORY OF ONE

But that one is hard to explain for your age.

WELCOME TO BEING HUMAN

My child, **THIS** is the shape of ALL THAT IS!

PART 2 – THE STORY OF ONE

But why are there always Seven and Two hidden?

*Oh, my child!
There is a simple
answer!*

PART 2 – THE STORY OF ONE

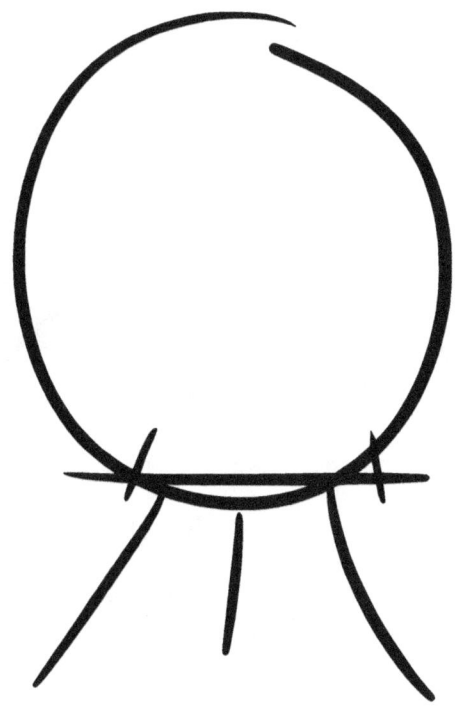

First think of a mirror...

WELCOME TO BEING HUMAN

...and now your reflection.

PART 2 – THE STORY OF ONE

Can you see behind your head?

WELCOME TO BEING HUMAN

or the other side of the mirror?

PART 2 – THE STORY OF ONE

THIS, my child, is like The Seven and Two Hidden!

WELCOME TO BEING HUMAN

Everything you see on Earth is a mirror...

PART 2 – THE STORY OF ONE

... of something inside of you!

WELCOME TO BEING HUMAN

So be LOVE and

full of WONDER!

PART 2 – THE STORY OF ONE

So everyone will know *you* see **LOVE** in the mirror!

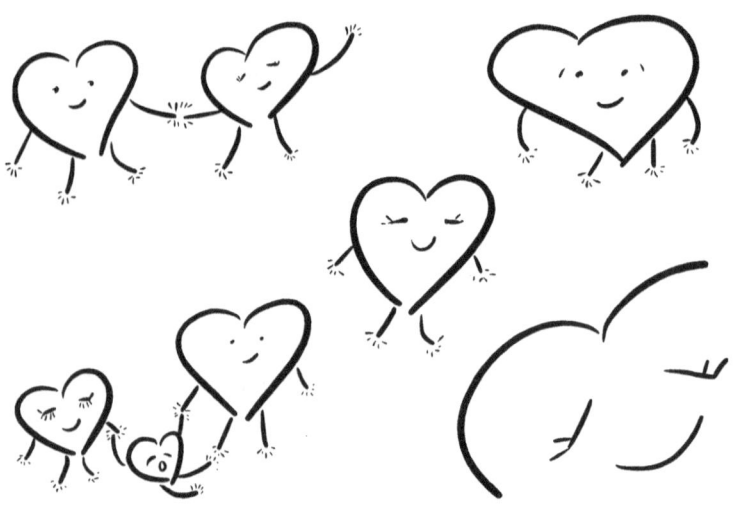

You Are Love, my child, *the One,* and so is ALL of Creation!

Welcome, my child, to being human!

Part III: What is Love?

PARENTAL NOTE: This story can be read by most children of reading age. It is intended to be read *TO* parents.

{ 3 }

For A Child To Read To An Adult

Love.

WELCOME TO BEING HUMAN

What is **Love**, my child?

PART 3 – LOVE

Love is like a big hug!

Love is warm like the sun!

PART 3 – LOVE

Love does not...

...want what another has.

WELCOME TO BEING HUMAN

Love does not steal or take from anyone.

PART 3 – LOVE

Love does not hurt anyone or anything ...ever.

Love does not judge...

PART 3 – LOVE

... since everyone is remembering how to be **Love.**

WELCOME TO BEING HUMAN

Love *always forgives* even when it hurts.

PART 3 – LOVE

Love can never be shown, given...

or shared through force.

WELCOME TO BEING HUMAN

Love can never be used to control others.

PART 3 – LOVE

If a human wants to control another human, it is not **Love** my child.

But above all...

PART 3 – LOVE

Love never-ever — *absolutely never* — has an agenda.

Becoming Love is Being Human!

{ Heart }

Postface

On Planet Earth…

Each of these stories was told for the world to see the very same story in very different ways. And surprise! This story is the same as the adult copy of this book! Oh, my child, there's only Love… and that is what you now know!

Welcome to being human!

www.ingramcontent.com/pod-product-compliance
Lightning Source LLC
Chambersburg PA
CBHW021157080526
44588CB00008B/387